Postman

What sort of life does a postman lead?
If you're out delivering letters and parcels in
the morning, you get up early and finish
just after lunch. You go on your "walk"
by foot, cycle or van. But if you're in a
sorting office you might work a different
shift. In the most modern sorting offices you
have automatic machines, like ALF.
Postcodes help you speed the mail on
its way. Postman drivers work with a
huge fleet of vehicles. It takes quite
a few to collect and deliver the
35 million letters and parcels posted
every day. Experienced postmen
trace mysterious addresses on
letters and parcels and take
charge of the registered mail.
In this book you'll see for
yourself what a postman's
life is like.

Choosing a Job

Postman

Tony Ford

Wayland Publishers

In this series

Frontispiece: Emptying the mail from postmen's collection into a segregator, which divides letters from packets.

ISBN 0 85340 345 7

Second impression 1975

Copyright © 1974 Wayland Publishers Ltd
49 Lansdowne Place, Hove, Sussex

Set in 'Monophoto' Univers Light
and printed offset litho in Great Britain by
Biddles Ltd, Guildford, Surrey

Contents

On the walk

Early in the morning

What is it like being a postman on delivery? You take your letters and packets out on the morning "walk". At most houses and flats you just push them through the letterboxes.

From time to time it's somebody's birthday, though. As a postman you can tell, because you might get a dozen cards for one person. Children come rushing to the door when they see you coming. It's good to see them getting excited as they rip open the envelopes.

If you do the same walk for some time you get to know the people you deliver to. If there are old people at an address, it almost becomes part of the job to keep an eye open — to make sure they are keeping well.

You have to be up and about early in the morning. It is cold and dark in the winter. But the fine fresh spring and summer mornings make up for that.

Early in the morning you are not the only one around. There's the milkman, the baker and the paper boy. You cross paths with each other regularly.

Unlike the paper boy who has to go off to school after he's finished his delivery, your job is over at about lunchtime. You can go home and put your feet up if you want to. Most other people are only halfway through their day!

Postman on delivery

The postman has to start very early to deliver your morning mail — usually between 5 and 6 a.m. He goes to the sorting office. There he collects the letters he is to deliver along his round or "walk", as he calls it. But before he starts his walk he spends about 45 minutes on an important job called "setting in". This is arranging his letters in order of delivery. He will have the right letter ready as he comes to each address along his walk. In towns and cities

the postman is sometimes taken to the starting point of his walk by van. Or he goes by bus. After delivering all his letters he goes back to the sorting office. He has a rest and perhaps something to eat. Then he goes out again on another delivery of letters or parcels. After that, at about lunchtime, his work is finished for the day. He has the whole afternoon to do what he likes, while other people are still working.

Through the letterbox

The postman on his walk sees hundreds of letterboxes. Nothing unusual perhaps. One letterbox seems much like another. But no, far from it. Every postman knows letterboxes are all shapes and sizes. He doesn't like the ones with flaps much too strongly sprung which trap fingers. Or letterboxes too small to take even an ordinary envelope. Or too narrow to take even the tiniest package. Then the postman has to knock and wait for someone to come and take the mail. That holds him up. If no one is at home the letter has to be brought back again on another delivery. You also sometimes find letterboxes in strange places. Some are only inches above the ground. Others are too high up. The postman has to bend or go on tip-toe.

Perhaps the designers of these houses thought an oddly-placed, tiny letter box with a strong spring looked smart. But it doesn't help the postman. Come to think of it — what is the letterbox like at your house?

Postmen aren't the only ones who have letterbox problems!

Postman's equipment

You have seen the postman carrying his letters in a bag or pouch over the shoulder. Sometimes the bag becomes quite full. But it would be unfair — and even dangerous — to expect him to stagger along with a huge load. So no postman is asked to carry more than 35 pounds (or 2½ stone) when on his delivery. Postwomen are not expected to carry more

Postmen's bags are not too heavy.

than 28 pounds (or two stones). As well as his uniform and cap the postman is given a mackintosh for cold or rainy weather. At night or on dark winter mornings it is difficult for motorists to see postmen walking or riding along. It could be dangerous and so the postmen wear white cap covers and white raincoats. They also have reflective armbands and reflective strips to put on their bags. Then motorists can see them quite clearly.

White clothing for dark winter mornings.

Postman in winter

In winter, roads and paths become icy and slippery, especially in the early mornings. The postman has to walk carefully to keep from falling. To help him keep his feet the Post Office thought of putting studs or tiny chains on the postman's shoes. With these he can grip the ground, even in ice and snow. In some parts of Britain postmen have been trying out

You have to take care walking about in winter...

...But chains like these stop feet slipping.

different kinds of equipment to see which works the best. Some have tried out specially studded overshoes. Others have worn gum-boots with studs in the soles. Others have small chains that fit under the heel and sole of the postman's shoe. So far, chains seem to be the best idea. Luckily winters in Britain are not often very bad. Otherwise the postman would have to wear snowshoes — or even skis!

Collecting the mail

Your postman not only delivers and sorts the mail. He also collects letters from postboxes and takes them back to the sorting office. This is done several times a day. You probably know where the nearest postbox is to your house. But the postman has to know where perhaps a dozen or more postboxes are on his collection round. In fact there are more than 100,000 postboxes in Britain.

People often dash to get their letters into the box to "catch" the post. Perhaps it's the last collection of the day. People sometimes post a letter by mistake when they're in a hurry. But the postman can't let them take it out of the box. Once letters or parcels have been posted that's that. They must stay with the postman and the Post Office until they are delivered. Think what would happen if anyone could just make up an excuse to get back letters from the post that were not theirs.

Dressed for work

Many years ago postmen's uniforms were very grand compared with the smart grey suits which they wear today. Between the years 1793 and 1855, for example, postmen wore splendid uniforms. They had fur hats with gold bands and a cockade, scarlet coats with blue lapels and cuffs, blue waistcoats and brass buttons. Later, in 1855, the scarlet coats were changed to blue. But, surprisingly, no trousers

Postmen's uniforms in 1855 were very grand . . .

were issued with them. The newspapers of the day poked fun at the postmen and showed them striding along wearing their coats over their nightgowns! After this the postmen soon got their trousers. As the years went by the uniforms became more simple in style and the main colour was dark blue. About five years ago they were changed to the grey suit-like uniforms worn today. Postmen get them free. They are longer wearing and easier to clean than the old uniforms.

. . . compared with today's smart suits.

Sorting the mail

Working indoors

Postmen work mainly out of doors. But there is still a lot to be done inside. Letters and parcels have to be sorted so that they can be sent to the right addresses all over the country. Most postmen spend some time working in

Machines like these sort letters automatically. In this picture, postmen are taking sorted mail out of the machine.

But there is still a lot
to do by hand.

the sorting office either before they go out on
their delivery walk or when they return. The
sorting office is the postman's headquarters.
Because there is so much to be done, some
postmen work there all the time. More and
more machines are built to help the postman
sort the mail more quickly and easily. But
there is still a lot to do by hand.

Sorting – in all directions

In the sorting office letters and parcels pass through in two directions – inward and outward. Inward mail comes from other sorting offices to be delivered in the district. Outward mail is collected in the district and is sent on to other sorting offices. The outward mail takes up the most work. First the letters and parcels

Every letter must be postmarked.

Then sorting can begin.

have to be postmarked (or cancelled) to show that the right postage has been paid. Next they are sorted, according to their addresses, into divisions — such as counties, large cities, or London districts (like EC1 or SE12). Then they are put into bags and sent by road or rail to the next sorting office. From there they are delivered. Inward mail is, of course, already postmarked when it arrives. It only has to be sorted into the addresses that the postmen find on their delivery walks.

ALF – The postman's friend

All newly posted letters are postmarked or cancelled before they are sorted. Then the first class letters and the second class are put into two groups. This is to speed up sorting the first class letters. First of all, the letters are put into a pile. Their addresses are on top and the stamps in the top right-hand corner. The letters can then be quickly postmarked and separated into first and second class. Usually the postmen do this by hand. But now there are machines called ALFs (automatic letter facers). ALFs do all three jobs – facing, cancelling and separating – at the rate of 20,000 letters an hour. ALF whisks letters along tiny conveyor belts. Special electronic beams spot which way up the letters should be. The belts twist and turn the letters the right way up. The beams also spot the value of the stamp and can tell whether the letter should go in the first class or second class group. ALFs are working in many large sorting offices. Eventually most postmen-sorters will have mechanical facing equipment to help them.

Inside ALF – rows of
rollers and belts

Inside—busy
activity.

A sorting office
"team" includes
postmen, drivers,
sorters and managers.

In the manual sorting office

Some sorting offices do not yet have many machines to handle the letters. They are called "manual" offices. This means that most of the work is done by hand. Where there are many machines the sorting office is known as a "mechanized" office. All sorting offices are very busy. They are always very well lit and are warm in winter. They are pleasant and friendly places to work in. The postmen work with each other every day and get to know one another quite well. In manual offices there is a steady buzz of activity, the sound of rustling letters and the thump of bags and parcels being moved around. In the mechanized offices a busy chatter is made by the machines. But the noise is not so loud as the roar of heavy machinery inside many factories.

27

Each letter goes into a box with a name above it.

Sorting — by hand

To sort the letters by hand the postman sits or stands in front of an upright sorting frame or "fitting", as it is called. It is honeycombed with 48 small open-ended compartments or "pigeon holes". Each compartment has a name on it — perhaps a county, large town or city district. The postman reads the address on each letter and puts it into the right compartment. All letters for Manchester go in the box marked "Manchester"; all those for Scotland into the "Scotland" box, and so on. Then the letters are taken from the boxes, put into bags and sent on to another sorting office for delivery.

Letters to be delivered locally are sorted into a different fitting. Its boxes have names of streets or blocks of flats or offices on them. The sorters are very quick at putting the letters into the right compartments. But, of course, they get plenty of practice!

A light has traced the sorter's hand in this special picture.

28

Travelling post offices

Travelling post offices are special railway carriages fitted out as sorting offices. As the trains speed along postmen in the travelling post offices sort letters. The letters are put aboard the train in mail bags. Sorting the letters as the train goes along saves a great deal of time. When the train arrives at its destination the letters have already been sorted into bundles ready to be delivered. The postman who works on the travelling post offices is a volunteer. That is to say he offers

Mail goes aboard a travelling post office.

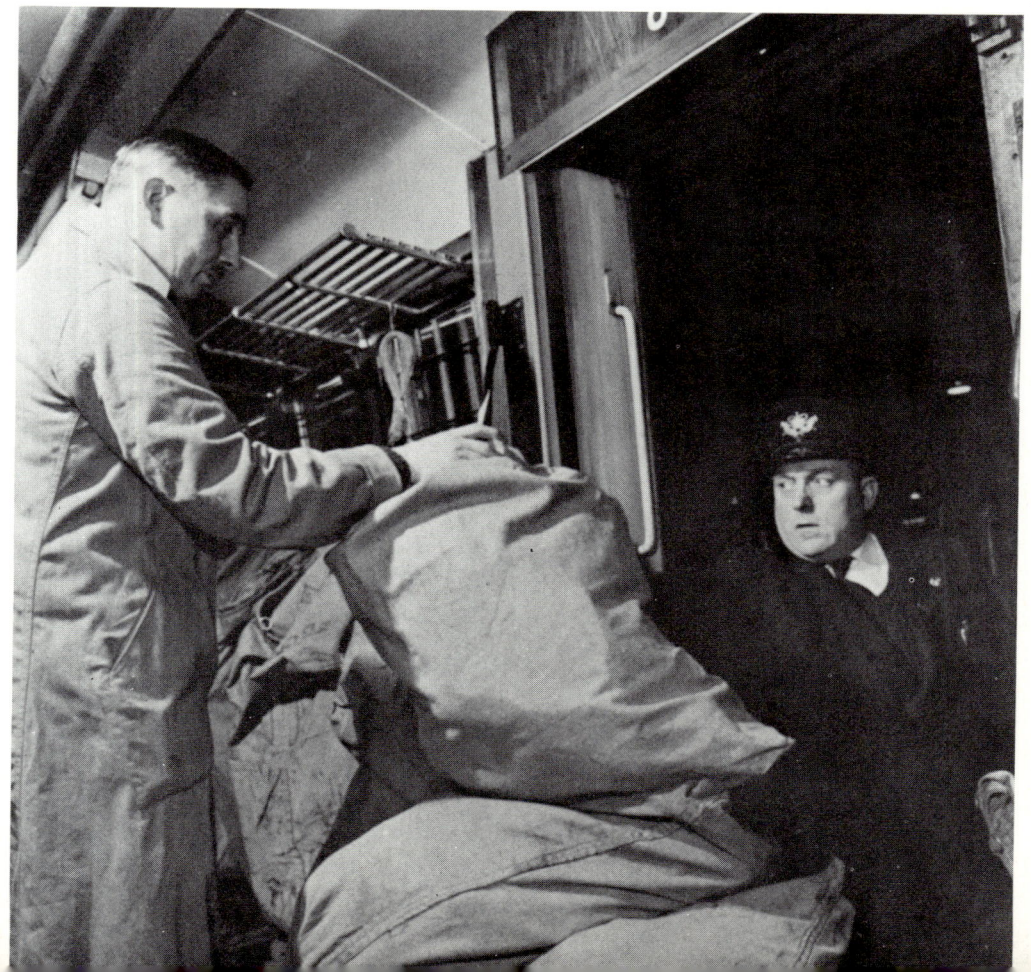

to work on them. It is up to him to decide because the working hours are often different from the usual postman's job. The postman who works on the travelling post offices may be away from home for two nights. He might travel north or south on the train for one night, sleeping next day and going home on the train at night. But one day the travelling post offices may not be needed. Special machines are being made which help sort the mail very quickly. Even postmen sorting letters as the train goes along cannot do the job as quickly as the machines in the ordinary sorting office.

Speeding along — with postmen sorting letters.

The code-breakers

Postmen are not secret agents, of course. But they know all about very important codes written on millions of letters today. The codes are called postcodes. They are a series of letters and numbers at the end of an address. LONDON W1A 1AA or IPSWICH IP3 3PS The postcodes help machines sort letters automatically and quickly. Your address probably has its own code already. All the 20 million addresses in Britain are being given postcodes.

How do they work? In sorting offices with automatic sorting machines, postmen read each postcode and type it out on a special machine. The postmen who do the typing are specially trained. Working at the postcoding desks is quite a skilful job. When the postcodes are typed out, rows of dots are printed in a special, almost invisible, ink cn to each envelope. The sorting machine can read the dots. Its electronic "mind" recognizes their pattern as an address. It sorts the letters into their proper pigeon holes at high speed. One day almost every letter with a postcode will be sorted at some point in its journey by these machines.

Left The dots are printed by postmen who read the postcodes.

Right An address turned into dotted "machine language".

Miss Wendy Brown,
500 North Street,
CROYDON,
CRO 9LA.

Parcel sorting by hand

Parcels are sorted several times on their journey after they have been posted. In many sorting offices the postmen do the sorting by hand. They look at the addresses on the parcels and drop the parcels into different bags according to the addresses. To do this they use what is called a "drop bag fitting" — a row of bags draped on metal frames. Each bag has a plate over it. The plate shows the name of the town

Left Parcels are put into "drop bag fittings".

Below Containers, packed with parcels, move mail quickly.

or county where the parcel is being sent. You can see this in the picture.

The postman works quickly, using his eyes and hands to put the parcels into the right bags as fast as he can. Each full bag is taken by van or train to another sorting office in the town or district where the parcels are to be delivered. In this second sorting office the parcels are put together ready for the delivery rounds. Sometimes the drop bag fittings are used again. But usually the parcels are put into big baskets on wheels called "skips". The skips are wheeled to the vans and the parcels loaded on to the vans. Today more and more parcel sorting offices have big machines which help postmen sort the parcels even more quickly. You can find out how the machines work from page 36.

Parcel sorting – by machine

The latest type of parcel sorting office has some amazing machinery. The machinery sorts parcels and moves them through the office. In a control room there are buttons, warning lights and TV screens on which the controller can watch the parcels going round the office. To sort the parcels, postmen read the address and press buttons on an electronic panel. This tells the machinery where to send the parcel.

Space-age control in a modern parcel sorting office.

Parcels pile up on special chutes.

The postmen push the parcels on to moving conveyor belts. From the conveyor belts the parcels fall down chutes into the right sorting compartment. Here other postmen put the parcels into a bag or metal container. The parcels are then either sent to a parcel sorting office in another town or taken out on delivery. More and more mechanized parcel sorting offices are being built. One day most of the postmen who sort parcels will have machines to help them and to take the hard work out of parcel sorting.

A postman's life

The postman's round

Up and down the country there are 100,000 postmen at work, day and night. They collect, sort and deliver the 35 million letters and 700,000 parcels posted every day. That's quite a few letters. If you could imagine all those letters piled on top of each other, the pile

Postmen deliver to 20 million addresses.

They drive a huge
fleet of vans.

would be 38 miles high! On their rounds in town and country the postmen between them deliver letters and parcels to 20 million different addresses — and yours is one of them. Postmen also drive vans and lorries carrying the mail. They travel by trains in special mail coaches, sorting the letters as they go. The postman is proud of his job. He knows that Britain has the best postal service in the world.

Left Loading night mail at London airport.

Round-the-clock postmen

The postmen's job goes on at all hours of the day and often through the night. The millions of letters and parcels are kept moving non-stop. The postman who delivers your morning mail starts work very early — often at 5 a.m. But he finishes for the day soon after lunchtime. Other postmen then take over and work until early evening. In some large sorting offices, or at railway stations or airports, postmen work at night. Every postman works for 43 hours a week but he is, of course, paid more for overtime. There is also extra pay for working at night, weekends or during holiday times. Postmen do shift work. They do not all work at the same time in the day. Some work in the

Mail on the move —
with postmen at the
wheel

morning, some the afternoon, and some at night. Not many postmen mind working shifts. After all it is rather nice to have your day's work done by lunchtime — or not having to start work until the afternoon or evening.

Above A goalmouth tussle in a Post Office soccer cup final.

Postman at play

A good thing about being a postman is that you get plenty of chances to enjoy your favourite sport or hobby. The Post Office has a lot of sports and social clubs for its workers. Name almost any sport or hobby and you will find it not far away at a Post Office club. There are local and even national Post Office championships in many different sports. Standards are often high. Post Office people have represented Britain in the Olympics.

But even if you are not interested in sport there is still plenty to do. You can take part or help out at Post Office social clubs, discos, youth clubs, motoring clubs and, of course, stamp collecting clubs!

You may think that the postman's favourite sport is walking. In fact many postmen are good at it. Each year a team of postmen from Britain competes against others from all over Europe in a race called the Postman's Walk.

Postmen — out of uniform this time — racing in the annual Postman's Walk.

43

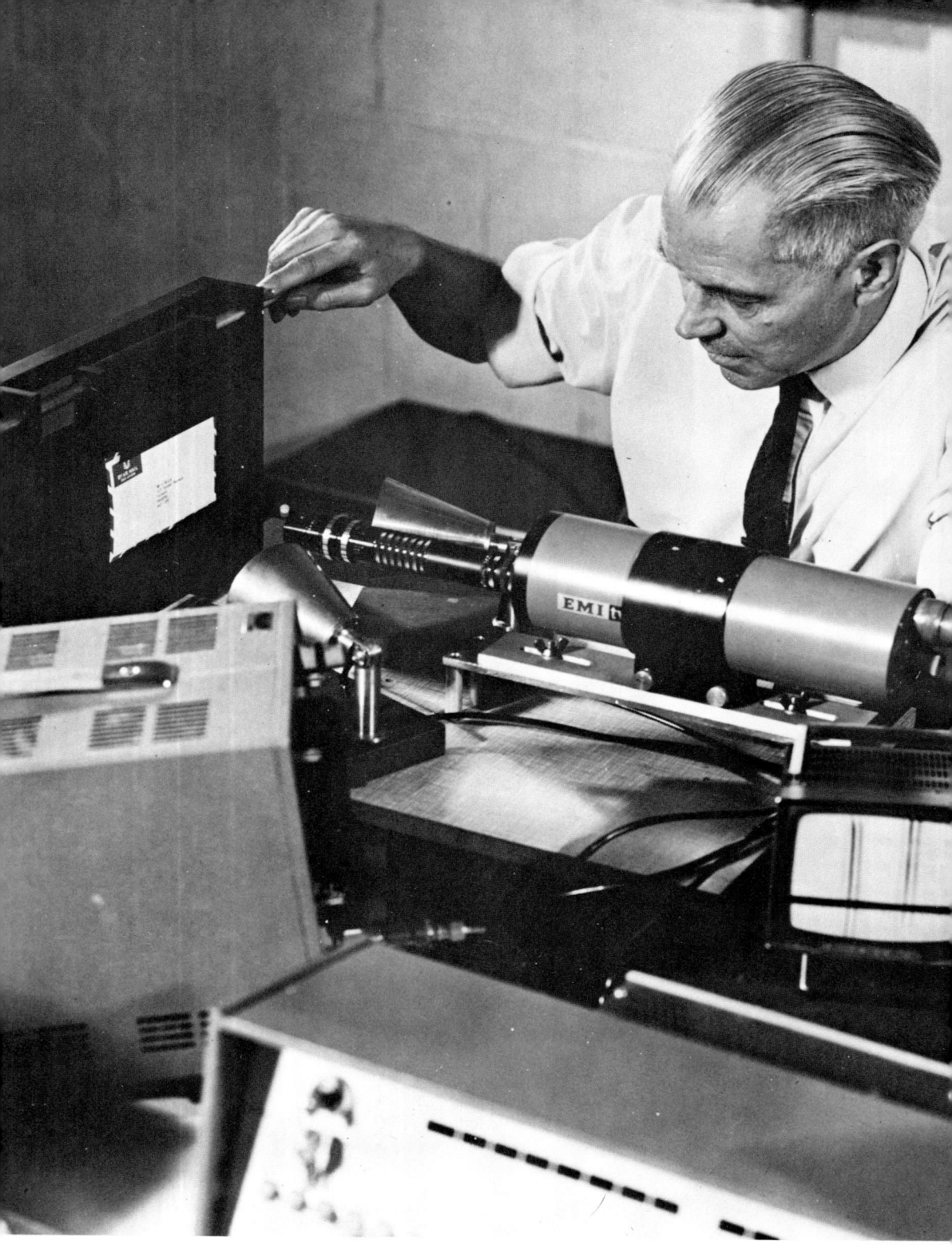

44

Machines may one day read addresses.

But the postman will always be needed.

Postman's future

There will always be jobs for postmen. One day there may be machines that can actually read addresses on letters and parcels as well as sorting them automatically. But this will take many years to happen. Even then the machines will only be able to help the postman — they can never take over from him. After all, the human postman will always do a great many jobs far better than any machine or even a robot. What comes naturally to the postman on his round — opening a garden gate, walking up paths, climbing stairs and putting mail through the letter box — would quickly baffle even the cleverest of robots! In fact the postman will be needed just as long as people go on writing letters. And that probably means for ever.

Two crowns on the lapels pick out the Postman Higher Grade.

Promotion – the first step

When a postman has learned his job well and is experienced he may then become a Postman, Higher Grade. This means he will get more pay. But he will also do more important work in sorting and handling mail. For example, one of his jobs is to see that registered mail is properly sorted and delivered. People register their letters when they want to post valuables, money or important documents. They pay a fee and fill in a small form when they post the registered mail. The letters or packages are then marked with blue crossed lines and get special attention on their way through the post. The postmen can see from the blue markings that the contents are important. When the postman delivers registered letters the people at the address sign a receipt. Then the Post Office can be sure they have arrived safely.

46

The postman's boss

The man in charge of a postman is called a Postal Executive "C". These men are rather like managers. They see that the work in the sorting office and on the postmen's delivery walks is done properly. Above them, Postal Executives "B" may be in charge of hundreds of postmen and a large fleet of vehicles.

The Executives "C" help organize the hours — or shifts — that the postmen work and arrange the jobs that they do. If you decided to become a postman an Executive "C" will inter-

These Postal Executives look after more than 1,000 postmen in one sorting office.

view you; he will tell you more about the Post Office and see if you are right for the job. The Postal Executives also help deal with badly, or wrongly, addressed letters. They handle any complaints or questions from the public about the mail service. The Executives "C" have years of experience. They were all once postmen themselves before being promoted. Of course, they have their boss too, the Head Postmaster. He is in charge of several sorting offices and postal districts. If you became a postman you might one day be a Postal Executive.

From the 625-foot
Post Office Tower
soaring above
London's bustling
streets . . . to a lonely
winding track out in
the country. Wherever
people live, postmen
are needed.

Right The feed belt of
a segregator. The
segregator separates
letters from packets by
means of a drum which
slowly turns round.

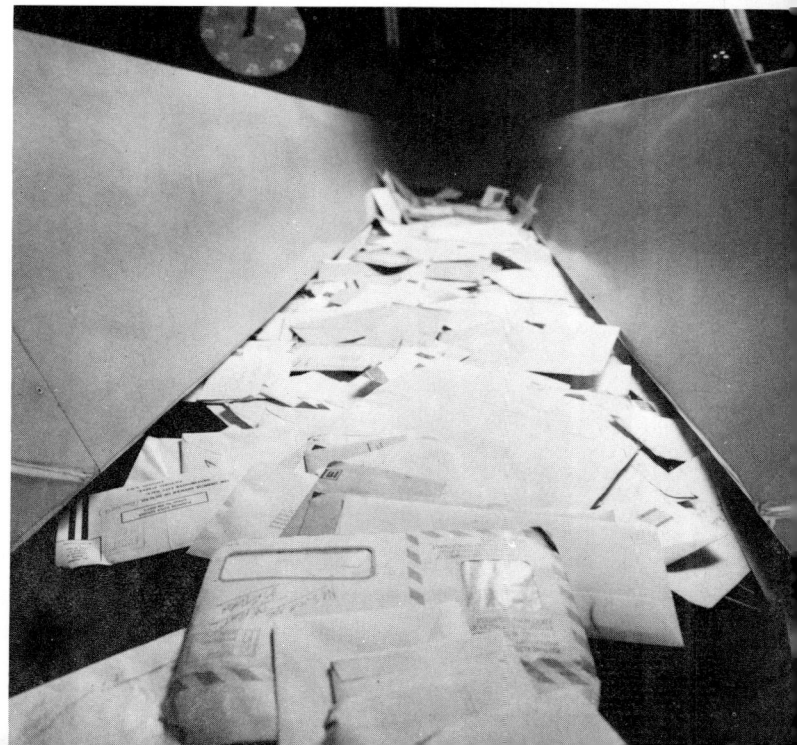

Postman plus

Behind the wheel

How can postmen collect and deliver the 35 million letters and 700,000 parcels posted every day? They use a huge fleet of 25,000 vehicles — one of the biggest motor fleets in

Postmen get extra money for driving.

Left Training at a Post Office driving school.

the country. There are mopeds, motor cycles, thousands of vans of different sizes, large motorway lorries and even small electrically driven trolleys. In country districts where roads are rough some postmen drive Land Rovers.

You could become one of the many postmen-drivers. When you are driving, you get extra pay. The Post Office often teaches postmen how to drive. Some postmen are full-time drivers, especially on the larger vans and lorries taking the mail to and from the railway stations, docks and airports. Many may drive thousands of miles a year. In fact the whole postal fleet travels more than 270 million miles a year!

Postman in the country

As a country postman you have a very different delivery "walk" from the postman in the town. You have to travel further between houses or villages. It would be too far for you to walk, so you use a bicycle, moped, or van. Your deliveries can take you many miles. You might visit lonely farmhouses or even houses halfway up a mountain and along rough and narrow tracks. Like some country postmen, you may even use boats or drive across causeways at

Even boats are needed to deliver the mail

low tide to reach people living on islands. In bad weather you might battle through snowdrifts or floods to deliver the mail.

In many out-of-the-way places it is hard for people to get to a post office. So you take supplies of postage or savings stamps with you for the people to buy. You also collect and post their letters and parcels or buy postal orders for them. You get to know the people on your walk far more than a town postman does.

Off the beaten track for this country postman.

Postman — bus driver

If you were a postman in some country districts of Britain, you would be a bus-driver too. Then you drive a mini-bus instead of a van and carry passengers as well as the mail. You travel between the towns and villages collecting and delivering the mail in the postbus — as it is called. But you also stop to pick up and put down passengers along the way.

The postbuses began running about six years ago because many villages today do not have ordinary bus services. This makes it very difficult for people without cars to travel into town to go shopping or visit friends. The postbuses run in ten country areas — in the Lake District, Wales, Scotland, Devon and Kent. There the people meet the postman and his postbus to get a ride into town and back again.

All aboard the postbus.

Clearing up problems

Will every address
be correct?

Baffling addresses

"The Proprietress, cream postal order shop
and groceries and sweets (on corner), bottom
of Pound Street, near sea front car park, by old
gun, Lyme Regis, Dorset."

This puzzle was an actual address on a letter
posted recently. It is just one example of the
thousands of strange addresses that people
write on their letters and parcels. Postmen
have to solve these puzzles. In this case the
sender did not know the proper address so he
tried to give some clues. There are many other
strange addresses. If you were a postman
would you know the answer to this address
seen on another recent letter? — The Civic
Society, Ciremaster, Gloo, England. (The
answer is at the bottom of the page.)

The Post Office spends more than £3 million
a year and the postmen work patiently for
hours trying to deliver wrongly addressed
mail. No wonder they are always glad to see
correct and clearly written addresses.

Busily sorting — and
some addresses are
very odd!

Answer: The Civic Society, Cirencester, Gloucester-
shire, England. (The letter was delivered without
delay!)

Christmas postman

Christmas is the busiest time of the year for the postman. He has to help deliver tons of extra Christmas cards and parcels. In fact at Christmas time more than 900 million letters and cards and more than 12 million parcels are posted. The regular postmen need help to cope with all these extra letters and parcels. About 100,000 people get jobs as temporary postmen over Christmas. Often they are students on holiday from school or college or old age pensioners. Perhaps you know someone who has been a temporary postman. The nice thing about being a Christmas postman is that people are very friendly. They are

Many willing hands help move Christmas mail.

always pleased to see the postman bringing the cards and presents.

Also at Christmas the Post Office hires an extra 6,000 vans and lorries to carry the mail up and down the country. Places such as parish halls, town halls and meeting rooms are turned into temporary sorting offices until the Christmas rush is over for another year.

But these presents must be packed again.

Wrong addresses —
searching for clues.

Mystery Mail — Part 1

Every day thousands of letters and parcels are posted with addresses that are wrongly or badly written. The postman then has to turn detective . . . "Is that a 3 or an 8?" . . . "Is that name meant to be Mr. Brown or can it be Mr. Bowen? . . . "Could it be Park Street or is it Back Street?"

The postman on his delivery walk can often see if a simple mistake has been made in an address. He can still deliver the letter to the right place. But when an address is obviously very wrong the letter goes to a part of the sorting office called the "dead letter" section. Here postmen, higher grade, search street directories or telephone books to find clues to the right addresses for the "dead letters". They are very clever at solving these problems. But still about 100 million letters and parcels every year cannot be delivered because the addresses are quite wrong or because the people at the addresses have moved away. What happens then? The next instalment in the mystery mail story is told in Part 2!

Another postman's
problem — badly
packed parcels.

Mystery Mail — Part 2

When postmen, higher grade, in the sorting
offices cannot trace wrongly or badly written
addresses the letters or parcels are returned to
the senders. If the sender's address s not on the
outside of the letters or parcels they have to be
opened. The postmen do not pry but just look
for a return address.

 With a letter, if a postman cannot find a
return address and there is nothing valuable in
letter, it is destroyed. All other letters and all
parcels are sent to a special department called
a Returned Letter Branch. Here more attempts
are made to find the sender. The letters and
parcels are filed and stored to wait for a claim.
Depending on what is inside, this mail is kept
from three months up to a year. If, after this
time, an item hasn't been claimed, it is sold as
lost property at an auction.

Mystery Mail – Part 3

Mystery letters and parcels go to one of the seven Returned Letter Branches in various parts of the country. Inside, rows of shelves and tables are piled high with the mystery mail – and the many different objects found inside. These often come from parcels which have been badly packed. On their way through the post the parcels have split and the contents have fallen out. If they can, the postmen or postmen, higher grade, re-pack the parcels But sometimes the parcels have fallen apart

Glum faces as mystery
mail objects pile up.

completely and the sender's address is lost too. The contents are then kept with all the other undeliverable letters and parcels at the Returned Letter Branch, waiting for a claim from their owners.

Every so often unclaimed objects are sold. These sales may have as many as 50 different items. There have been umbrellas, golf balls, watches, frying pans, dolls, all kinds of presents — even Christmas trees and turkeys. Once a box of live spiders was found in the post. When their sender could not be found the spiders were given to a zoo!

Starting as a postman

Becoming a postman

Every year in Britain 6,000 more postmen are needed. They take over from men who have retired or moved to other jobs. Extra postmen are also needed in towns or districts where the amount of mail to be handled is growing. More postmen are probably needed where you live. The employment exchange, the youth employment office or your school's careers teacher will tell you. Or can you write to the local Head Postmaster.

If new postmen are wanted and you apply, you take a simple written test, followed by an interview. Postmen do not have to have GCE or CSE passes. Instead they take a test to show that they are alert enough to do the postman's job. In the interview you will be told more about the job. You will have another chance to show that you are keen and bright. If you pass the written test and the interview, you will soon be starting your first day as a postman.

New postmen at a training school learn about the latest parcel sorting machines.

Taking the test

If you want a job as a postman, you have to take a written test. It isn't difficult. The test for the young postman is very much like the one for the adult postman.

First you are shown some examples of the kinds of questions in the tests. Here are some:

Underline the two words with the same meanings — happy, surprised, motionless, timid, still. (Answer: motionless, still.)

Underline the two words with opposite meanings — near, early, probable, annual, late. (Answer: early, late.)

Another question tests whether you can check accurately. There are two columns of names and addresses which look the same at first glance. In some, deliberate mistakes have been made. For example: Mrs. H. A. Davenport, 18 Abbey Road, Oxford; Mrs. H. A. Davenport, 8 Abbey Road, Oxford. You can see that in the second address the number has been changed from 18 to 8.

There are also simple sums, including fractions and decimals. (Such as $12 \times \frac{3}{4}$ and $4.25 + 6.5$.)

You'll have plenty of time to answer the questions.

A test for Young Postmen

In this test you are given sets of instructions. You have to read them and then write down exactly what they tell you to write.

Examples

		Answer
1	Write down the first word in this sentence which begins with t, and has at least four letters in it.	THIS
2	If EIGHTEENTH has more E's than SEVENTEENTH, write down the total number of E's in both words. If not, write down the first letter of the word with most E's.	S
3	Write down the seventh letter of the alphabet unless it comes after F, in which case write the fifth letter of the alphabet.	E

test for Adult Postmen

This is a test of commonsense and observation of everyday things, and lasts 20 minutes. Each item has four drawings and you have to indicate which drawing answers the question.

Example

| A | B | C | D |

Which picture is wrong ?

The answer is B, because the bicycle chain goes to the front wheel instead of to the back wheel.

Young postmen

You can become a postman at 16. Until you are 18, you are known as a "young postman". You work mainly as a special messenger delivering on foot, cycle or motor cycle, telegrams or urgent letters and packages. Many young postmen also help deliver and collect mail within the Post Office's own departments and head offices. You have time-off on full pay to go on studying at college, if you want to. Studying has helped many postmen to move on to other jobs in the Post Office — perhaps as managers, sales executives or

Looking and learning on the first day.

experts on mechanization. At 18 you become an adult postman. You move on to the full range of jobs such as sorting letters and parcels, and going out on your own delivery walk. All postmen (including young postmen) work a total of 43 hours a week with extra pay for working in London or for driving. There are three weeks and three days paid holiday a year plus another $8\frac{1}{2}$ public and Bank Holidays (such as Easter Monday or Good Friday). Almost all sorting and delivery offices have their own staff restaurants. Young postmen are given vouchers to help towards the cost of their meals.

A nineteenth century young postman.

A new postman
(Britain's tallest at over
seven feet) is shown
his first delivery walk.

Learner postman – the first day

Your first day as a learner postman – like your
first day at school – will be a bit strange. There
are new faces, new buildings and new things
to do and learn. But you always have someone
with you to explain the job. On your first few
days as a young postman, you are shown
around by one of your workmates. But it is not
long before you are on your own – travelling
on foot, cycle or motor bike delivering
telegrams or urgent letters. Some young
postmen may find themselves working in a busy
Post Office department. There they help with
the collection and delivery of mail for various
offices and senior staff. Most of the time young
postmen work with people of their own age.

The new adult postman gets more detailed
training on such things as sorting the mail
and getting it ready for delivery. He then goes
on delivery with an experienced postman. In a
very short time the new postman is going solo
– out on his own delivery. After a few weeks
he may have more training – sorting letters to
places like Perth, Penzance and Pontefract or
San Francisco and the Solomon Islands.

Postal terms

Automatic letter facer   Machine that arranges letters the same way up (facing) so that they can be cancelled quickly.

Datapost   A special door-to-door postage service for packets carrying documents or computer tapes. Datapost packets are specially looked after as they pass through the system. You can send by Datapost now to America, Brazil and Europe.

Dead letter   When a letter has a wrong or strange address it is called a "dead letter" and put on one side. Later the postman tries to find its right address.

Drop bag fitting   Frame on which a bag is hung and into which parcels are sorted.

First and second class mail   First class mail costs more and is delivered more quickly than second class mail.

Fitting   Row of small boxes into which letters are sorted.

Freepost   Companies who advertize and want people to reply put FREEPOST in their address and the replies can be sent free. The companies pay a fee to the Post Office to pay for the postage on the letters they get.

Manual office   Sorting office where most of the work is done by hand.

Mechanized office   Office with many automatic sorting and cancelling machines.

Philatelic Bureau   Philately means stamp collecting. Stamp collectors all over the world who want to buy British stamps get them from the Post Office's Philatelic Bureau in Edinburgh.

Post Office Railway   The Post Office has its own private underground railway under the streets of London. It carries mail between the main sorting offices in the city.

Postbus   In some country places mail vans on delivery also carry passengers.

Postcode   Series of letters and numbers at the end of an address (e.g. LS1 9TD); machines can "read" the code and sort letters automatically.

Postmark (cancel)   A date mark on each letter so that the stamp cannot be used again.

Recorded delivery   When people want to be sure a letter has been delivered they pay a small charge. The postman gets a signature to show that the letter has been delivered.

Registered mail   Important mail. It travels in specially marked envelopes so that it is well looked after. When it is delivered the postman gets a signature as proof of its safe delivery.

Returned Letter branch   When letters and parcels have very odd addresses or when the people to whom they are addressed cannot be found, they are sent to Returned Letter branches. There the postmen spend many hours trying to trace the correct address.

Separating   Splitting letters into first and second class bundles.

Setting in   Arranging letters in delivery order.

Skip   A large basket on wheels used to move letters and parcels around the sorting offices.

Telegram   Short, urgent message passed by telephone, printed on a form and specially delivered. A telegram message takes only hours to deliver from start to finish.

"Walk"   Postman's delivery round.

Young Postman   Young men can become postmen at 16. Until they are 18 they are called Young Postmen. They mainly do messenger delivery work, telegram delivery, etc.

Finding out more

If you want to find out more about the Post Office's postal service and about jobs, write to the Head Postmaster of the area you live in.

You can get other information, including schools project help, wallcharts, posters, etc., from these two addresses:

Postal

    Schools and Recruitment Section (PMk4),
    Postal Headquarters,
    St. Martins-le-Grand,
    London, EC1A 1HQ

Telecommunications

    Education Service,
    Publicity Division (TMk3),
    Telecommunications HQ,
    2—12 Gresham Street,
    London, EC2V 7AG

If you are interested in British stamps, in getting the new issues or the monthly Post Office Bulletin for collectors, write to:

    Post Office Philatelic Bureau,
    2—4 Waterloo Place,
    Edinburgh, EH1 1AB

Index

Picture credits
The author and publishers would like to thank the Post Office
for all the illustrations in this book.